Our Journey Is
Our Work

Izzy —
It is a pleasure to have you as part of our journey!

12/16/06

Our Journey Is Our Work

Creating My Obituary

A Guide to Personal Growth

Russell R. Shippee

iUniverse, Inc.
New York Lincoln Shanghai

Our Journey Is Our Work
Creating My Obituary

iUniverse books may be ordered through booksellers or by contacting:

iUniverse
2021 Pine Lake Road, Suite 100
Lincoln, NE 68512
www.iuniverse.com
1-800-Authors (1-800-288-4677)

ISBN-13: 978-0-595-40349-3 (pbk)
ISBN-13: 978-0-595-84724-2 (ebk)
ISBN-10: 0-595-40349-2 (pbk)
ISBN-10: 0-595-84724-2 (ebk)

Printed in the United States of America

With gratitude and love I dedicate this book to my wife of thirty-five years, Cathy, and our children, Christopher, Erin, and Kathryn, who have all been my greatest teachers and supporters.

Contents

Prologue

A role as God's messenger is not what came to mind when I thought of myself prior to age fifty. Nor is it what most of my friends would say of me today. Yet, we are all messengers.

This book is you, and it is me. Yes, you will find yourself, like it or not, in this book. Yes, we are in denial, and we self-medicate to avoid looking within.

While my friends and family will be surprised by this book, my wish is that it inspires and provides insight for all of us.

If you have picked up this book, there is a reason you have done so. I'd suggest reading it. If you resist reading it or resist it while reading it, please know that that is a message for you. If you put the book down, keep it, as at some unknown point in the future you will want it.

In 1988 my mother wrote me two notes, which she received as automatic writing. Automatic writing is a gift from the other side that provides messages to assist people on this side. She did not know what the notes said until after she wrote them. I kept the notes but paid no attention to them until 2002. Then, when I was ready for the messages, they rang true and clear.

The note of January 13, 1988, told me I was healed in the spiritual and had to slow down, clear the mind, breathe deep, stop judging others, and allow the healing in the physical. The message also said that tension blocks healing, and one cannot push the body too hard. I was to let go and let God. On April 30, 1988, a second message was given, politely advising me that I had failed to follow the first message and must do so for my well-being. In 2002 I sure did take the notes to heart and followed them as best I could. In hindsight I wonder what took me so long.

When referring to one's higher power, I use the word "God." Substitute the word(s) that you desire.

My beliefs come from my mother, her automatic writing, books, discussions with others, the Bible, and my life experiences. I state them as facts, as they are facts to me. Interestingly, they all come back to simple principles. Some are provable, some can be seen and felt, and others my intuitive self tells me are correct. At times words do not do justice to a belief that can be felt and known.

The foundation of my belief system is:

- We are all one.

- What we do to one we do to all.

- What we do to another we do to ourselves.

You do not have to agree with me. Please read and consider. Allow for the possibility. Work with it and live with it. At some point, it may become your belief system also.

No, I do not live my beliefs; I *try* to live my beliefs. I succeed more often than I used to and, ideally, less often than I will tomorrow. Together we are all students.

My close friend, Jaime, calls me "the new kinder gentler Russell." He is quick to remind me when the old Russell is responding.

You will get out of this book what you put into it. Please read this book again and again. Each time, you will gain knowledge and take away a new and different perspective.

Creating My Obituary

"In my beginning is my end…. In my end is my beginning." T. S. Eliot

What was your birth like?

Hidden in our subconscious is the story of our earthly birth. On a conscious level we learn about the experience of our birth from our parents. I was the second twin, born about thirty minutes after my brother. I was small, had undeveloped lungs, and stayed in an incubator for a few days after my brother went home. Apparently I was short of breath during delivery. Now I believe the delivery was a frightening event and that I was left alone to recover without the love, affection, or touch of parents in my first few days. What effect, if any, has this had on my life? Has this haunted my relationships since then? Why do I sometimes forget to breathe?

Today you might call my childhood family "dysfunctional," as most are considered to be. My mother was an alcoholic, and my father an enabler as well as a workaholic. My mother would fall off the wagon and drink, drive, and attempt to do her motherly duties. My father appeared to avoid the issue and buried himself at the office. As a family, we never discussed alcoholism, nor were we ever told it was a disease. As kids we were embarrassed, afraid, and never discussed the problem among ourselves. You just did not talk about family problems, within or without.

At age seventeen I met Cathy and was smitten. After five years of dating and thirty-five years of trauma and drama, I still am. She was the first person with whom I ever discussed my family and feelings. When I have been willing to talk, she has always been there. Now I know she was a guide sent to help me. In the beginning she was just a great-looking girl I was chasing. It has taken me a life-time to learn how much more than that she is.

Our parents did the best they could. As we all pick our parents before we are born, and as there are lessons we need to learn while on earth, my parents were, accordingly, teaching me. Perhaps we should be thankful rather than hostile about our parents as we grow and develop. Do I know and understand all my lessons? No. If I did, I would no longer need to be here on earth. Our parents are mirrors to us. When we dislike something in the mirror, it raises the question of whether we dislike something in them or in ourselves.

At about age seven I remember wanting to be a minister. However, I was told a minister doesn't earn enough money. To this day I do not know who told me that or how I came to that conclusion. Although I really wanted to be a minister helping people, I changed my sights to business so I could earn a good living. At age fifty I decided I wanted to go back and help others in a new and more mean-ingful way. Money was no longer a satisfying goal. A feeling, a knowing, was growing within me that my life was to be more than money, and a new way, helping others, would be my mission. I was bored and dissatisfied as an insurance agent.

I had studied accounting in college and then joined the family insurance agency. I was the fourth generation in the agency, bought the business from my father, and expanded it substantially through acquisition of other insurance agencies, as well as adding new clients. It was my job to honor the heritage and pass it on to future generations. It was my obligation.

A vivid dream changed me. I had died, and my casket was at the front of the church. The minister stood in the pulpit saying, "He was a great insurance agent." I knew that was not the legacy I wanted to leave, and if I did not leave the business it was going to kill me.

I sold the family insurance agency during its 100th anniversary. Selling a family business is emotional, due to the history and the perceived obligation to carry on. It was expected that I would continue it. While I legally owned the agency, my father still had moral control. Although my father understood and had given me permission before I sold it, he was upset after it happened. "I worked for the agency for sixty-two years, and my son sold it and fired me" was his mantra for several years whenever I was within earshot. Had I given myself permission to accept this criticism?

I had raced through life without enjoying relationships to the extent that I should have, without providing enough quality time with my children, and without spending enough quality time with my wife, Cathy, and close friends.

There were cars, boats, and real estate. It was all stuff that took time, energy, and money. It was just stuff whose purpose was to feed my ego. I was climbing the wrong mountain.

While we did travel and owned a ski house in New Hampshire, the family escapes were never complete. I was always tired, grumpy, and preoccupied, as well as connected to the office by telephone. My family and friends never had my full attention or energy. I had lost the spark, the fun, and the creativity.

During the early 1980s we would give New Year's Eve parties in New Hampshire. However, the highlight of the night, for me, was when the office faxed the year-end profit and loss to me around 10:00 PM. I then went to bed exhausted while the others enjoyed life and one another.

What did feel great and satisfying was being involved in worthwhile organizations. I was the president of the Providence Ronald McDonald House and head of the capital campaign to build the house. Rhode Island Hospital was building a children's hospital, and I was asked to raise funds and then asked to join the hospital board. Several years ago South County Hospital asked me to join their board and I am now chair of the capital campaign to raise money for a new bed tower. Giving back and serving these worthwhile organizations was most rewarding and satisfying. Putting my business experience to use in building was much more rewarding than buying more things.

Success, and what it cost, held a valuable lesson. Was it worth the price paid? We keep repeating lessons until we learn the lesson. For me, chasing the money and position was no longer worth the price. The cost is in time not spent with loved ones, relationships not developed, and health problems. The cost is in not doing what you are meant to do.

Work fills time and allows us the luxury of not looking within to find our true selves. Work is like self-medication, administered so we don't have to look at the pain or the hurt. Eventually one stops or is stopped by illness and is forced to look, see, and evaluate. This is a difficult time.

Unbeknownst to me, my first big message came when our daughter, Katy, was diagnosed with cancer at the age of two and a half. The suspicion was confirmed with an operation to biopsy a tumor on her lower spine as well as to remove the parts of the tumor that were accessible. The technical term was a ganglioneuroblastoma. We were told it was cancer and then allowed to see her in intensive care.

In an instant our lives changed forever. Our little girl was deathly ill, attached to life support, and looked so small and helpless around all the intimidating equipment and people. Time stopped. Our lives stopped.

In just over a year Katy underwent three sets of chemotherapy, three major operations, and radiation. The hospital was our home. This period was a wake-up call for us. We were learning the true value of life, love, and family. We found support, love, and amazing doctors, nurses, and caregivers, as well as other parents in crisis. There were victories and tragedies shared by many of us. We had entered a world of which we knew nothing.

"Will you come home and go for a bike ride with me?" was the telephone call from Katy the day after one of her many hospital stays. Life had offered an opportunity, and I could not miss it. I immediately left the office and went home for a bike ride with my daughter. It felt terrific. As I rode around the neighborhood, I thought to myself, this is what love and life are all about.

My second message came when, at age thirty-eight, I developed a kidney problem known as membranous glomerulonephritis and blood clots. "Don't get up," the doctor told me as I started to come to after a procedure. "You have a blood clot and cannot get up for a few days." My world had stopped for the second time. "My family needs me, I can't let them down, the office can't run without me, I need to be strong, this is not fair, what do I tell Cathy, why am I crying, I can't let Cathy see me crying" were the thoughts racing through my mind. "I have no control" was the most frightening thought.

When I was fifty-two, the kidney disease relapsed, as I had yet to pay attention to the messages. While I had sold the business, I was racing to find my new mission. Finally, being forced to, I slowed down and let my body heal as I looked, worked, and studied within. Illness is a strong message and a powerful tool that can force us to try to look within. Illness can be a dual gift: the right to slow down and the time to do so.

While sick I remembered and reread two messages my mother, who did automatic writing, had given to me when I was thirty-eight. Automatic writing is when someone is compelled to write something and they do not know what it says until after they have written it. It is considered a message from the other side of consciousness. The messages were timely. Of course, it sure would have been better if I had paid attention the first time! Time was running out for me, and I finally realized it was now or never for this life experience.

During this period of illness and recovery, I had time to review my life and my life lessons. Sure, I would have done many things differently, and I would have treated people differently. I would have respected people more, given people more time, and been more tolerant and far less judgmental.

I was always too quick to judge and criticize. Rather than listening and understanding someone's point of view and reasoning, I was judge and jury without all the facts. After all, facts can only undermine confidence in your own misinformed belief system. My respect of others was hidden with my quick judgment and failure to give them the time required. My tolerance was nonexistent, as it had been obliterated by exhaustion and stress.

Yes, many things would have been different. However, that is the case with most of us. The past is for learning from and not for regrets. Our past years were perfect in that we received what we gave. Actions and reactions were perfect. If we are dissatisfied with our past, we should be joyous about what we have learned and what we are now aware of. All we have is the *now*, and we can live the *now* better having had these past experiences. Ideally we won't continue to make the same mistakes.

I was climbing the wrong mountain of ego, money, and power. I was operating out of fear of rejection, fear of not being good enough, fear of not fitting in, and fear of making less than my neighbor. The mountain was fun and exciting, and then suddenly it became boring and barren. "He who dies with the most toys" no longer seemed such a laudable goal. Now I am climbing a new mountain that is exciting and awakens me with energy and enthusiasm. I do not know how many mountains are ahead of me during this earthly lifetime. We need to find the right mountain for ourselves. That does not mean following what others tell us to do, what our family expects, and what pays the most money.

Our inner work becomes real when we leave the security of a job. We may have sold our business, been terminated, quit from boredom, or retired. We may have been forced through illness or some other trauma to take the time to look at ourselves. We are given a gift of time that may feel like a curse.

The inner vision, the inner understanding, the inner work can't be done at a desk or within a given timeframe. It is all-encompassing, all-consuming, and takes all our time. It can be the most difficult time. It can be a time of feeling no connection. It can be a time of lonely empty feelings. It can be a time of fear. It is the fear of the unknown, the fear of looking at oneself, the fear of not knowing what is next. While these fears are real, they create value by focusing our attention, learning, and understanding.

The mountain we climb changes. As we grow and develop, our needs, our lessons, and our mission can change. Mine is changing from money, power, and ego to assisting others. Others change from a dead-end job to taking the risk to do what they enjoy. Others follow their creativity rather than suffer in a desk job pushing papers. Crisis and tragedy lead many people to find a driving passion they want to follow for the good of others. Follow your heart's desires, and when they change you also can change.

Cathy has been and is my crutch and security, which, truth be known, I have taken for granted. She is the one who supported and did the behind-the-scenes work so I could run the business and be on nonprofit boards.

My heart, my guides, and my intuition led me to write this book. To do so I had to face my fear, bare my soul, risk ridicule, and show the world what I was doing. Will the book sell? Will anyone read it? Will anyone get something out of it? I trust the answers will all be yes.

The end of the story of this life on earth is also the story of a new beginning. At the end my obituary could list all my roles, my jobs, and the clubs I belonged to. However, that might not reflect the real value of my life. I would be proud and humbled to have an obituary as follows:

- He was a loving and caring husband.

- He was a loving and caring father.

- He was a loving and caring grandfather and great-grandfather.

- He was an author.

- He taught, helped, encouraged, and motivated others to be the best they could be.

- He served for the good of the community.

- He left the world a better place.

We Are All One

"Resentment is like drinking poison and then hoping it will kill your enemies."
Nelson Mandela

We are all one. We are interconnected. We are light, we are vibration, and we are all that is.

On earth we feel we are all separate individuals. That is wrong and creates a basis for separation. The idea that we are separate creates much of what is not working as it should be in our world.

We are all one. What we do to one we do to all and we do to ourselves. What we give out comes back to us. When we fight, we get fought. When we kill, we get killed. It does all balance out.

When we love and honor, we are loved and honored. When we see the good in others, they see it in us. When we lose ourselves helping others, we find ourselves. When we respect, we are respected.

We are one, and we are God. We are all there is. Being light and vibration we see, know, and feel. How else would you explain that we can often know what someone is thinking? How else can you explain thinking of someone and then they call you? How else do you explain that we just connect and are in sync with someone? Coincidence?—I don't think so.

Part of our journey is taking on a body and experiencing this dream called life on earth. The learning also involves realizing we are all one with all that is. We are connected to the source of all that is and to the information and answers of all. Realizing this, we can be one with all that is and make the world a better place.

What good has any war done? What has been the value of killing others? Who are you and I to impose our views and values on others? We can kill, and we can force people, but we cannot win their hearts and minds with this behavior. Force and destruction do not win people. No war has ever done that. The true value is in the hearts and minds of people.

The winning is in knowing we are all one. The winning is in respecting others and working with them. Know we are all one, and we are viewing things differently, but the end goal is the same. We are all here for lessons. It is not for us to change the world as much as it is for us to learn our lessons and allow the others to learn theirs.

We choose how to live this life. We can get into the fray of forcing others, or we can assist them in learning from a positive position. Remember that you can catch more flies with honey than with vinegar.

Death Is Birth—Birth Is Death

Is birth a wonderful, joyful, and miraculous event? What about for the baby being born? Does the baby have the joy in seeing us that we feel in seeing the baby? Or is it like what we conceive the torture of death to be? Is the baby coming to the light and wonder of earth or coming to the darkness?

Our earthly life begins at birth and ends when our physical body dies. Birth is not the beginning but a stage in our soul's evolution, and our body is a container to help us learn the lessons for which we have come to earth.

It appears at times that birth has great pain because of a baby's crying, and conversely death can be peaceful and natural. One could ponder the question of birth being the big trauma and pain, while death is the natural act and evolution. Death is just the elimination of the physical container and a return to our soul's more natural environment.

We are born by choice. We decided to return to earth to learn and accomplish our life's work. Most of us do not know why we chose to return, and we spend a lifetime trying to find out. We will learn, and we will grow. However, it will take a long time and many lifetimes, depending upon the choices we make while on earth in these physical bodies.

Life is not just here on earth in a physical container. It is much more than that. This temporal life is just a small part of our life and evolution.

Die now so that you know there is no death. Die now so that you can engage in earthly life without fear. There is nothing to fear.

Life and death are part of the process and part of our being. We are eternal. Our spirit exists on many levels. We are energy; we are vibration; we are light. We are all one.

Transition

Transition is our soul taking on a physical body or leaving a physical body. Transition is birth as well as death. Transition is going from one form of light and vibration to another.

What is our world? What are we? Our world is light and vibration. The rate of vibration determines the density. A rock appears solid to us as it vibrates at a low rate. Humans vibrate at a higher rate and appear to be less solid. There is much we cannot see. We on earth can only see within a limited range of vibration.

The transition of a loved one has a great value for those left behind. We feel the pain and joy of a loved one leaving us. We feel the void. We feel the pain of a relationship temporarily lost. We are able to better appreciate those who are still with us. We have an opportunity to understand what our relationships mean to us and to understand the value in expressing our feelings while the people are still here.

In losing, we gain. We gain wisdom and appreciation. We gain time to be alone and quiet time to look within. These times have great benefit for us and our personal growth. However, they are also difficult times. Looking within is not easy, and we do our best to avoid it.

Losing a loved one feels like losing part of ourselves and leaves an empty place in our life. It could be that the person provided us with support and did things for us that we are not prepared to do or qualified to do. The person may have been our biggest fan and the one who gave us courage and strength.

Losing a loved one also brings out and shows us the support and love others have for us. In times of loss and need, we find support and love from friends. This support and show of emotion and compassion is a great lesson for all of us. It is a glimpse into the true nature of God within.

The loss of my mother showed me love, respect, and caring from others. Simple things such as a telephone call, a hug, a pat on the shoulder, as well as a look of compassion and understanding, meant more to me than I had realized they would. I saw the good and the person beneath the social mask. Some reach out while others, you realize, cannot, in spite of the look in their eyes that says they wish they had the strength and ability to do so.

When our daughter, Katy, was sick, we were amazed. Some close friends reached out and others hid. We were surprised and confused. Finally we realized those who appeared to hide were just not able to express themselves. They are good people who were just not able to reach out.

Do not judge others that you expect to assist and support you when they do not. Deep down they want to, but they are not able to understand how to do it. Reaching out to them will help both of you. Holding a grudge will help neither.

Years ago a friend lost his son. When I was ill he reached out and took me to lunch. I was amazed when he told me how much our words and support had meant to him in his time of loss. One never knows the good they have spread by treating people the way they would like to be treated.

Our perceived loss is a gain for others. It is a gain for those on the other side awaiting our loved one's arrival. The one we lose can help us from the other side without our knowledge. We will gain when we transition over, and the loved one awaits us. As the Quakers say, "Listen for the silence"—this is often where the vibrations are the loudest.

Why on Earth?

Why were you born? Why at this point in history? Why have you suffered and prospered? Why have you been treated fairly, unfairly, or with favoritism? Why, in your viewpoint, is your body thin, fat, ugly, or beautiful? Why were you born into poverty or wealth?

Everyone's perception is their reality. Everyone's reality is a little different from everyone else's reality. Who is to say who is right or wrong? From our own perspectives, we are all right.

Your birth was not an accident but part of a plan you made to return to earth. You chose your parents, your body, and the timing of your reentry to earth. This plan was based on the lessons you need to learn and perhaps a karmic debt to be paid. While here, most are not aware they made a choice to come back. You are now advanced enough to realize that you are here for a purpose and that you chose in advance that purpose and the surroundings in which you need to learn.

Earth is a school, and lessons will keep repeating until you learn them and move on to new lessons. We are to learn, grow, and develop here on earth. We come to advance, and we come to work toward a higher spiritual plane. We come to pay debt and to help others. We agree with other souls to assist them and return with them. Our assisting might mean hurting them physically or emotionally on earth in order to assist them.

We may come to earth with disabilities that show and teach others or to learn and experience ourselves. We may come to help another reach a goal. We may come to learn and have others come to assist us. We may suffer an untimely death to help those left on earth learn. Perhaps we will do something wrong so that others will see, realize it is wrong, and not do it themselves.

Is it fair? Here on earth it may not look correct or fair. However, when back in the spirit and reviewing what happened on earth, it will all make sense. It is not for us to judge while here on earth. We do not know the full story. We must realize all is as it should be. We attract our future based on what we do today. Small changes made today can have a huge impact on our future. Taking a new course, starting a new job, moving, or making a new friend can lead to a new and different life as time proceeds.

Most of us must work to sustain ourselves or to maintain the family. We think of work as something we do for money, for our families, and for our ego gratification. Work is what is necessary to care for our bodies as well as to provide food and shelter. However, the main purpose of this work has more to do with relationships with people—learning, growing, and interacting—than with the issue of money earned or product made.

Looking back at our various employments, we usually have good as well as bad memories about people and our interaction with them. The memories are more about people and accomplishments than the money. While I am no longer in the insurance business, some of my close friends still are. While I no longer work with them, they are still friends and we still talk and get together years after we worked together. They taught me valuable lessons and are still teaching me. Today I can see more clearly that what appeared to be just a frustration was really guidance and of value. These people who appeared to be roadblocks were in fact stepping stones to help me gain understanding.

Perhaps our language and perception are wrong. Work seems to have a negative connotation to some. It shouldn't. Work and play are both activities. Both work and play can be fun and rewarding. Work and play teach us and allow us the opportunity to be with others and learn from them, as well as teach them. It is all about relationships, compassion, and love for all.

Work can be considered the classroom or framework for learning. Work can be an office job, a farmer's job, or a homemaker's job. Work can be satisfying or dissatisfying.

An office job can be fun, due to interacting and assisting others. It can also be torture, just processing papers in a cubicle, for those who need to be outside and moving around. A farmer's job can be a breath of fresh air and exciting to those who love to work with the earth and grow things. That same job can be torture to a person who does not like the heat or cold or getting one's hands dirty. I know some women who found great joy and creativity in being a full-time mother. Others needed to express their creativity in a career as well as being a mother.

On earth our journey is our work. Our work is not only the job that brings in a paycheck but also all that we do and the lessons we learn.

We are here to learn, grow, assist others in their learning, pay karmic debt, love, and to realize we are all one.

Fear

"Do that which you fear and the death of the fear is certain." Mark Twain

Fear is an emotion, a feeling, a reaction, a mirror, a message, and also a warning. Fear helps us to learn. Ideally, we will learn there is nothing to fear. If you do what you fear, the fear will die.

Fear can be caused by:

- Abandonment (Will they leave me?)

- Acceptance (lack of) (Will they include me?)

- Rejection (What if they blackball us?)

- Separation (What if they want me to leave?)

- Self-Worth (lack of) (Am I adding value? Do I have value?)

- Surrender (Willing to trust the abundance to support you?)

- Trust (Can I trust my God to support me?) (Can I trust anyone?)

- Being Stuck (Why can't I make a decision?)

- Sickness (What did I do to cause my illness?)

- Incompleteness (Why am I not whole? What is missing?)

- Pain (Is my pain real, imaginary, physical, or mental?)

- Ignored (Why don't they see me standing here?)

- Concern for the future (What will happen to me tomorrow?)

Stop. Look again at the list above and write down one example of a personal experience of fear caused by each of the items. You will be amazed. It will be beneficial for you to review your personal examples hidden within your being. Notice how they affected all you did or did not do.

We can act out of fear, which is of earth, the mind, and the ego. Alternatively, we can act out of love and compassion, which is of God.

Fear results in jealousy, anger, and in our being, or trying to be, someone we are not. Remember someone you thought would perform better than you? Did you not want to somehow eliminate them? Instead of being true to ourselves, we are true to whatever we feel brings us acceptance and inclusion. Perhaps you dress in a way that you think is accepted rather than as you would prefer to dress. You might try to befriend someone you are not fond of so as to be included in a group. Fear keeps us from feeling good about ourselves and from doing what we want to or should do.

Fear prevents us from doing what we may feel compelled to do. I felt the need to sell my business and write. Will anyone understand me? Will they read my book? Will they understand it? All of these questions were in my mind as I took the leap to do what I felt I had to do. Fear prevents us from creating and living to our fullest. Fear of ridicule, rejection, and failure prevents us from taking action. Fear is paralyzing. When facing death, the biggest regret is risks not taken. Had I allowed my fears to stop me, you would not be reading these words today. Having done what I felt I needed to do, I feel fulfilled and alive.

Fear of loss or injury prevents us from living. Fear of not having enough money makes us work for money rather than fulfill our life's purpose. Fear of not having enough causes us to hold on and not share with others. To live the life I wanted, I needed to accept the risk of injury as I skied down mountains. I was willing to give up the paycheck to change and do what I felt had more value for me as a soul on earth. Sharing feels good and creates more. Only in the sharing can you see and feel the abundance.

Face the fear. Make your life as exciting, interesting, and creative as you desire by doing. It is your life, and you choose how to live it.

Ben Franklin said, "A few of the things I worried about actually happened." How many things have you worried about that never happened to you? How many bad things have happened to you that you never considered or worried about? How many things that caused you fear ended up being blessings in disguise?

First, we must confront fear and walk toward it. For me, it is this book and a new career. By not responding to our fear, we will find the fear loses all its power. Once I took the leap by selling the business, the fear subsided into excitement at what was being created. What is the worst that can happen? Death? Die now so you know there is no death. Life is eternal. There is nothing to fear.

Confidence

If you can believe it you can do it.

Confidence is a state of mind, a presence, a feeling. While you cannot touch or buy confidence, you can feel it and see it. Confidence, or lack of it, cannot be hidden. Confidence is for us all to see and know.

Confidence can be seen in one's face, walk, stature, actions, speech, and being. Confidence can speak louder than the clothes we wear or the cars we drive. Some people can make an inexpensive outfit look expensive by the way it is worn and the way they carry themselves. While the clothes and cars are symbols and tools employed to create an image, true confidence needs no earthly props. Gandhi is an extreme but wonderful example. Beware of false confidence parading as true confidence. Many people present themselves as confident, while inside they feel the same fear and doubts we have. We have all seen the high-flying con artist who ends up on the front page of the papers defeated.

Confidence is the lack of fear, as well as knowing who and what you are and living that life. This can be seen in the local doctor who quietly and effectively serves patients or the local teacher who humbly serves while mentoring so many. Confidence is having faith in yourself and not obtaining your self-worth from the comments and opinions of others.

Confidence is obtained by doing. Once you do something, you are more confident that you can do it again, and the more you do it successfully the more confident you are. For example, I have taken up sailboat racing. The starting line is crowded, and the sailboats do not have brakes to stop. The first year I held back and had no confidence. Once I started to do what I feared, my confidence grew race by race. Now, I am right in the middle of the action trying to get the best possible start. I look forward to the challenge and the opportunity to prove myself and do my best.

Confidence makes the difference between success and failure. Confidence gives one the focus and strength to do what one sets out to do. Knowing you can do something allows you to relax and do it while enjoying it without fear. Now I can win more races, as I do not lose time at the starting line. Winning one race leads to winning more. I now enjoy the race, the competition, and the challenge.

Can you remember attempting to do something, but fear prevented you from succeeding? Can you remember knowing you could do something, and then you did it in a relaxed manner?

Failure

"The men who try to do something and fail are infinitely better than those who try nothing and succeed." Lloyd Jones

What is failure? Failure is not obtaining the desired outcome. Failure is practice and learning. Failure is the process of learning. When learning to ride a bicycle, is it failure when one falls off?

Is failure bad? Is failure negative? No. Failure should be considered positive and rewarding. It shows we are attempting new things, learning, growing, and developing.

Failure is progress and learning. Failure is the elimination of things that do not work as you progress toward what does work. Failure is just a step on the path to success.

Was Thomas Edison a failure? He failed many times trying to develop the electric light. Finally, he found the solution. He is honored for the development of the electric light and the perseverance to keep testing until he found the correct solution. His attempts to find the solution were just steps in finding the answer that did work.

Was Olympic skater Scott Hamilton a failure? He came in last in his first national competition. He came in last more than once. The judges told him twice to leave the ice early as he had no chance. For Hamilton, being last was not a failure but instead a stepping stone to the Olympics. He was fired from the Ice Capades. Then he started the Stars on Ice tour which has been a success for years, while the Ice Capades is no longer in business.

Failure is what doesn't work when you are trying options to see what does work. Failure is a process to find what works. What works can be called success. Failure is a natural and proper progression of learning. We are here to learn, and learning is trying and doing. Failure is one of the steps we need to take in our learning process on earth.

I was not selected for a position once, and the person selected, in my opinion, was less qualified than I was. One could say I failed in that I did not get the position. The other side of the coin is that I wanted out, my plan had been to get out, and to have been selected would have been wrong and detrimental to me personally. In failing, I won. The failure allowed me to move forward to what I truly wanted to do.

Perhaps we should either redefine failure as noted above or eliminate the word from our vocabulary. Fear of failure has prevented many people from doing and creating for the benefit of us all. Ideally, overcoming my fear of failure in writing this book has resulted in a product that can help the reader. True failure is in not attempting the task or stopping before you succeed.

Friends—Enemies

"The only way to have a friend is to be one." Ralph Waldo Emerson

Is it you or me? Am I looking at a butterfly, or am I the butterfly? Why is he a friend today and an enemy tomorrow? Am I a friend or an enemy?

We are all one. We are connected. You are part of me, and I am part of you. We are both part of all others as well as part of the earth. Everything is connected. Everything is vibration, energy, and light. What we do to one we do to all.

Embrace all, as we are all one. Our perception of people is founded on a superficial, earthly basis. We have a friend or an enemy based on our earthly feeling about a person and how we have interacted. Most people who we respect and pay attention to think of us as friends, and we think so of them. It's all about how someone perceives being treated and respected.

Our friends may come to us in this life to assist us in our lessons and then become enemies so that we may learn. It may be part of the plan that is hidden from us while here on earth. It is not for us to judge friends or enemies but to learn, grow, love, and respect all. Remember, we are all one and do not know what another's lesson may be at this time. When back in the spirit, it will be clear to us, and we will then understand.

Remember the saying "keep your friends close and enemies closer"? Perhaps that is because our enemies teach us some of our most meaningful and valuable lessons. Our greatest tormentors might just be our greatest teachers.

"Why does God give you good friends?" is the start of the joke. The punch line is "to make up for your relatives!" Those relatives from hell are of great value. They represent lessons and relationships that do not go away. Who is to say that these relatives are the problem? Perhaps they feel *you* are the relative from hell. Could we be the problem? If I am honest with myself, I can see where I had opportunities in the past to correct rifts in relationships with family members before they got out of hand. If only my ego, my pride, and my judgment had not gotten in the way.

Relationships come and go. You use me, and I use you. I help you, and someone else helps me. We get together when needed and part when we no longer need each other. New relationships present themselves for new lessons. You can never love and lose. The fact that a relationship appears lost or forgotten does not mean it should be so. In life on earth, the relationship may be rekindled years later or may be lost until another lifetime.

"Till death do us part" is part of the wedding vow, as is "for better or for worse." Cathy has stuck by me and has grown and changed as I have. We are most fortunate. Spouses are always friends to each other, but at times they can sure feel like and act like the enemy. We all are playing off of and learning from each other.

The difference between a friend and an enemy is in the relationship. If we take the time to respect, know, and listen to other people, we will find reasons to like them and understand where they are coming from. While we may not agree, we can still be respectful and disagree at the same time.

If I had a relationship based on respect with someone, I could come to an agreement on a business deal. If I treated the other person as an enemy and did not build a relationship of respect, then I could never succeed in dealing with that person. First, we must listen and understand the other person. If we do not take the first step, the rest of the steps toward an agreement usually fail. The deal and the agreement are a by-product of respect and relationship and not of the agreement itself.

I used to feel good when I put someone down, beat them, and put them in their place. The funny thing is the feeling was short-lived. Then, when I needed them or needed to deal with them, I got back what I had given out. I was the loser, and I lost deals and money that could have been made. If I had understood this lesson when I went into business, I could have built a bigger business faster and with greater success. More important than the money would have been the additional relationships and mutual respect.

You may be wondering about several situations of your own that fit this description. Go and visit with the people, listen to them, understand their point of view, and respect them. Some of my best relationships today started on the wrong path, but I was able to save them. Make a friend first. Try it. You'll like it.

We see others whom we think are enemies. The problem is, we are our own worst enemy. While someone else might say or do something, it is not what the other person does or does not do. Many times it is our incorrect interpretation of what the other person said or did that we accept and believe. The other person may not be an enemy. The other person may not have meant anything negative. It is our assuming the negative when it was not the intention of the other person. We are our own worst enemy.

Forgiveness

"To err is human, to forgive divine." Alexander Pope

On earth we are here for lessons and experiences. They are perfect for us and what we need. However, in any given situation, our action and reaction may not be, in hindsight, perfect.

Many times we look back and wish we could take back what was said or have the opportunity to do things differently. We can and do look at others and judge how they have hurt us or our loved ones. They may have hurt us or shortchanged us. All of this is our truth and our reality.

We can hold grudges, negative feelings, and hostility. This hurts not only the other person but also hurts us and our bodies. Negative energy clogs us up and hurts us. The other person usually knows of our feelings without our even verbally expressing them. We are all energy and vibration, and others can feel that without our expressing it verbally.

The road to good health and a happy life is also the road of forgiveness. Perhaps, were we to look in a mirror, we would see ourselves, many things we wish we had done differently, and all those who have forgiven us. What would our life be if others had not forgiven us?

Have we not all harmed another? Have we not all felt the joy and release of being forgiven? Have we not all felt even better about those who were kind enough to forgive us?

Why do we not forgive? Why do we hold grudges? Why do we replay the hurt tape in our head? Why do we think of all the things we would like to do to them to get even? Why do we forget the joy of forgiveness?

While forgiveness is good for the other person, it is also healthy for you. Your health and well-being suffer when you hold grudges. Through the act of forgiving, you will find you gain as much as or more than the person forgiven. Your body will relax, your endless tapes will stop, and you will feel at peace. Forgiving frees you and makes you feel good again. You will wonder why you held such negative hostility. You are bound to appreciate the response of the other person.

In this way forgiveness opens the line of communication. You may discover the experience was not what you had thought it was. You may realize that you had made a wrong assumption about the situation and find yourself apologizing for it.

How often did your parents forgive you? How often has your spouse forgiven you? How often have your employer and coworkers forgiven you? Have you been forgiven far more than you have forgiven others?

Forgiveness is healing. Forgiveness is enlightening. Forgiveness is empowering. Do it for the other person, but mostly do it for yourself. You do more harm to yourself than you do to the other person by holding a grudge.

Yes, forgiveness can also be the difference in making a deal or not.

Guides

Who is guiding me? Who am I guiding? Are guides earthly beings?

Guides do not wear name tags advertising who they are. Many of them we do not know, and their guidance comes from our having hunches and just knowing. Others are here on earth and have physical bodies as we do. They can be spouses, children, relatives, close friends, strangers, employers, fellow employees, or an enemy.

New people show up in our lives for a reason. Things do not happen by accident. It may be long after a relationship has ended that we realize how it helped and guided us. In hindsight we realize what we learned and how we were assisted.

For me, meeting Barbara Cansino Kaufman was such an experience. She writes for the *New York Times* and wrote an article about going to Christ Church in Oxford for a summer writing course. I had to go. To my amazement, I met Barbara at Christ Church the day I arrived for my course. I saw a woman with a fun-loving smile who looked like an aunt I admired. We hit it off, and during a conversation with one of her friends, I was told she was the person who wrote the article in the *Times*. Barbara would have never told me or anyone. Months later she became a guide for this book. Without her this book would not be all it is.

Who has come into your life to guide you?

At times we may be guiding those who guide us. Being a guide is an ever-changing role. We are all guides to someone at some time, as well as being guided ourselves.

Guides are available and standing by to assist us. Guides are here for the asking. Asking is as easy as asking a question in a simple and direct way with the confidence that the answer will come. Then we continue our daily activity, knowing that when we are ready the answer will come. Guides are always with us and could be considered our sixth sense.

Remember when you just knew the right thing to do. Remember when you could have been hurt but were saved. Remember when you took the correct turn in the road but did not know why at the time. These are the times when a guide was with you. Your knowing was a guide assisting you.

"Take the boat out of the water today" was the message early one Friday morning when I wanted to leave the boat in and sail a few more times. The message was too loud and clear to ignore. It came from my mother, Virginia, and the boat is named Lady Virginia. I called and was able to get a time that day to haul her. The gear all had to be removed, and I was able to do it just in time. The last step was to tow the trailer to the boatyard in Cape Cod to leave her for winter storage. The rain started as I unhooked the trailer from the truck. The next week severe weather hit, including torrential rain, hurricane force winds, and cold temperatures.

Mirrors

What is a mirror? A mirror is our reaction to what we see in others. It is our reaction to what others do or say. It is what our filters show us from the interaction.

Notice how a person makes a statement, and later the same people who heard the same words can each have a little different slant as to what was said. The reality for the listeners is based upon their mirrors and filters as to what is said and what it means to them. We all have our own reality and reaction. That is why there are so many differences. That is why we all have different truths.

Our actions and reactions toward people provide a message to both sides. It is all about us and our reaction. We need to dig deep into seeing what our mirrors of others tell us about ourselves. It is us and not them. By our actions and reactions, we tell them how to treat us.

Other people are mirrors for us to help us learn. It is the mirror that teaches us and creates value for us in the lessons. It is up to us to step back from the stage of life and reflect on the lesson and the deeper meaning of any action and interaction. Whatever has an emotional charge also includes a needed lesson. What happens to us happens for a reason. Our interactions are for a purpose and should teach us something.

When we meet someone and like them, the meeting may be showing us something missing that we need or want. If we dislike someone, they may be showing us a trait of ours from this life or a previous life that we dislike and would prefer to avoid.

Mirrors are the messages we send and the messages we receive. We determine how we see things based on our needs, our filters, and our personal insight. We can find great value and learning in our mirrors.

My father is a great mirror for me. He never took the time to have lunch with clients and build personal relationships. One of my lessons has been to value lunch with others, and it is a source of enjoyment, friendship, and learning. He taught me well by much of what he did and also by what he did not do. The apple does not fall far from the tree.

Vibration

We are vibration. Earth, fire, wind, and water are vibration. Communication is vibration. Vibration is everything.

We vibrate within ranges. That is why most of us do not communicate with people who have crossed over. The only difference is the rate of vibration. We can only access within our vibration range.

We need to be in tune in order to receive. All is already known, and all is already created. It is just our access that is the issue and the limitation. Some can access more easily than others. Some just seem to know. Some get it, and some are not ready to get it.

Life is simple. Life is light and vibration. Remember when you felt you were in tune with someone? You knew what they were thinking, how they would respond, and what they would do. You could read their mind, and they could read yours. How did that happen? It was a vibration match. You were both on the same vibrational frequency. It worked. You could and did communicate without words. Words are not necessary for communication.

If we put ourselves into the right vibrational frequency, we can communicate with ease. We can accomplish much with ease. Life is more fun, work is not difficult, and much is achieved with little effort.

All questions are answered. We might not get the answers and will not if we are not in the right vibration frequency to receive them. Expecting, knowing, and allowing the answer is part of being in the frequency needed. It is our expecting and allowing the answer that makes the difference.

Why do answers come to us? Why does the answer appear when we are not focusing on it? Why do we get flashes of answers? It is as simple as being in the right frequency or allowing the frequency to access the answer already given. We need to relax and allow. We need to feel. We need to know the vibration and allow it without forcing it.

Being in the right frequency allows us access to the answers we seek. It is all there, and it is all available if we know how to access. The key is our vibration and allowing the vibration.

My mother was able to vibrate at a different level and do automatic writing. At times I just know things. I know the answer, I know what is going to happen, and I know what is right. It is not that I am smarter. It is that I allow the answer, I feel the answer in my being, and I get my mind out of the way so that I can feel and know it from a different place.

Being in tune brings to us what we need and desire. Being in tune allows us to know within our being what is right and wrong for us. It allows us to know what we are meant to do and accomplish on earth. Many times it is different from our ego-driven mind and the socially accepted path. But knowing it in our being is such that we cannot ignore it for too long. It comes back and reminds us until we change. Sickness and injury can come to slow us down, make us aware, and pay attention.

Once we slow down to know and to receive, we can then get more answers and more directions by accepting them. This grows and increases as we allow it. It is our vibration. It is as it is meant to be. We just need to allow it, feel it, and work with it. It is so simple that it seems too easy to be correct, but struggle blocks the answers. Allowing, feeling, and knowing bring the answers.

"Intuitive," "psychic," "lucky," and other words are used to describe people who know or get answers. The truth is, it is as simple as being in tune and allowing, as well as feeling, the answers. Answers coming this way feel right and provide confidence. Many times the answers are simple and common sense.

Our expectations create our vibration, and our expectations create our future reality, which is a self-fulfilling prophesy. Yes, we think, feel, and make our future, and much of it is subconscious. Whatever we focus on, we get.

Even focusing on what we do not want brings it to us. In golf if you focus on the water hazard, you will more than likely hit the ball into the water. We create the vibration match and bring to ourselves whatever we are focusing on—positive or negative.

What you think about and do is reflected in your vibrations. Expecting something and moving with confidence on it creates a vibration match that allows it to be. This is why affirmations work if properly written, reviewed, and believed. If one says and repeats affirmations without belief, they will not create the vibration match, and it will not work. It is that simple.

If we can allow the right vibration, the rest will happen easily and automatically. We will get our hearts desire. We will be able to do what we are meant to do. We will know what we need to know when we need it. We will be guided and assisted in all that we do and all that we accomplish.

Heaven or Hell

Is this heaven, or is it hell? Is it neither but something else called "earth"?

Where is heaven? Where is hell? Where is earth? Do we know the answers? How do we know? How can we be sure? Can we be sure?

Perhaps earth to us is what we make it. At times earth is heaven to us, and at times it is hell. What is the difference? Is it us? Is it what we do? Is it our perception? Is it our attitude?

Heaven and hell are concepts. They exist in our minds. At times we feel like earth is heaven when all goes well, all is beauty, and all is as we want it to be. Other times nothing goes our way, and everyone seems to be against us. Now, earth is hell.

We choose. We decide. It is up to us to choose. We can make earth heaven, and we can make it hell. It is our perception and how we live it. We get back what we give out. What we perceive becomes a self-fulfilling prophesy.

Let's choose heaven. It sounds better, and it is the goal for many. Why wait? Let's have heaven on earth.

First, we have to decide what heaven means to us. For many it is happiness, health, sunlight, brightness, goodwill, peace, and timelessness. It is the vast open area of the unknown where we go after we leave this earthly body. Some say it exists along with us just at a different vibration rate, which makes it such that we cannot see it. However, some can feel it and feel others who have crossed over.

Now that we've decided to make this heaven on earth, we can stop rushing, and we can stop judging. When we stop rushing, we realize we did not need to rush anyway. Life is better and feels a little like heaven. When we no longer judge, we are not judged. We no longer have hostility and grudges. We treat people with love and compassion, and we find we get the same back. Love and compassion make us feel like we are in heaven. We find peace. We find the good in all, which we had not been able to perceive before. We see good all around us. We accept and embrace the good.

With love, compassion, peace, no time, and no judgment, all is well. The haste and hostility of life on earth has ended for us. We only see and feel the good. The light is brighter. We feel alive and vibrant. We have released the chains of negativity, and we are free.

We no longer chase the gods of material things. We no longer have to work hard to acquire. We no longer have to try to impress others. We no longer have to try to beat others. We have time to help and enjoy others, and they help and enjoy us. Competition is gone and replaced by compassion. Selfishness is gone and replaced by sharing.

We are in the same physical space, but all is changed. All is as we have always wanted it to be. It is as we want it, and it is as we live it. We are with people who are like ourselves—we attract them, and they attract us. We have created our own heaven on earth.

By the same token, we can make it hell. We can fight and be fought. We can cheat and claw our way to more money and more things. Doing this will put us in contact with others doing the same. It will be a dog-eat-dog existence, without peace, love, and compassion. It is a life of separation and winning at the expense of the other person. It is not healthy, and our bodies will suffer with the stress and strain. Our success makes it hell. We create it and compete in it. We are blind to what can be, and we keep suffering. We complain, and we fight others. We are neither happy nor peaceful. Beauty escapes us as we rush from one thing to another. We race through life never knowing, truly knowing, another. We have no time to help and only time to try to beat the other person.

We all know people that can bring hell to our lives. I still judge others, get mad, and allow others to frustrate me. It even feels good to think I am getting even.

However, that feeling is short-lived, and I know we only hurt ourselves. For me, relatives are the biggest challenge.

We have a choice. We can pick hell and the games and competition of hell, or we can choose heaven and be one with all that is. We can share, support, and live with compassion. To choose heaven, we have to give up competition, separation, and judgment.

What do you choose? Why? What is stopping you? How do you start? How can you make this heaven on earth? Where is the instruction manual? Where is the coach?

If you choose heaven:

Slow down; stop; let go and let God.

Be compassionate to all.

Do not judge. (We do not know the full story, so who are we to judge?)

Accept all that is.

Know we are all one—live as we are all one.

Share—there is abundance for all.

Be kind.

Be welcoming.

Treat your neighbors as you want to be treated.

Enjoy and embrace the earth, the sun, and the sky.

Respect and honor others and the earth.

Find and celebrate the good in others.

You can do all these actions to create heaven on earth. You already have the skills. It is a matter of determination and desire. No, you may not be perfect. However, the better you get at it with practice, the more it will feel right, and the more will be given back to you. It is a win-win situation for you and all those with whom you come into contact. You will find this is heaven on earth, and you are the deciding factor. It is what you make it. It is your perception. It is your actions and reactions that make it so.

Perhaps the most interesting thing is that it is up to you. You choose. You make this life what you want it to be. Of course, you can keep the drama of the world against you, the world picking on you, the world hurting you.

You already know people who live as if this is heaven. They enjoy all that is and always have a smile, a warm greeting, and a good word for everyone. If they can do it, so can you. Sure, they have good luck and good friends that make the difference. That is because they created and attracted it. You can do the same. You have the same choice and the same opportunity. What are you waiting for?

Choose heaven. You will be glad you did.

Do What You Do Best

Do you use your God-given talents to assist others and make this world a better place?

When you were born, you were given unique talents. These talents are for you to use to help yourself and others. If you do not use your talents for the benefit of all, you risk losing them. Yes, we all have talents, but we do not all have the same talents.

Your talent—be it making money in business or playing musical instruments—will help you and others to grow and succeed. You can add new skills while helping others learn your skills. In working together and doing what each does best, the sum total will be greater.

We need to appreciate the skills others have that we do not. We need to respect what others can do. We are all equal, but our skills are different. Some people have the skill to cut a hedge perfectly, to build a stone wall, or to perform open-heart surgery. All of our skills are needed.

For me, process and flow of work as well as the principle of touching the paper only once has been second nature. In helping others, it seems so natural and easy to me that I wonder if there is value in it. However, in hindsight, the assistance is of great value for the clients who do not have that skill. We do what is easy for us and provide it to others for whom it is not easy. It is that simple.

Do not be jealous of someone else's skills. Use yours and develop them. You chose, in advance of birth, what skills you needed to accomplish your lessons. Focus on yourself and what you can do for others. Celebrate what you can do and share it.

Consider the famous actors and glamorous actresses. Do they have lives you covet? It appears that they cannot do much outside their homes without being caught in the zoom lens of the tabloids. Many have problems with drugs, alcohol, relationships, and feelings of self-worth. Just think of the tragic endings for Marilyn Monroe and Elvis Presley. Perhaps you are better off as you are. Perhaps you have more to be thankful for than you realize.

Regrets

"Twenty years from now you will be more disappointed by the things that you didn't do than by the ones you did do. So throw off the bowlines. Sail away from the safe harbor. Catch the trade winds in your sails. Explore. Dream. Discover." Mark Twain

Forget regrets. Regrets are for things in our history we wish we had done differently or not done at all. We cannot change what was done in the past.

We can change the way we view the past. As we grow and develop, our filters of past events change our perception of them. For me, I am thankful for my family and their issues. Having grown up in a dysfunctional family and worked with a workaholic, I am better able to help others who are having the same experience. Therefore, the past events have helped me and others. As we learn, we understand more.

We are here to learn and grow, and what we did in the past has helped us. While we might have done things we would not do now, those things have helped us progress to where we are today. A close friend never misses the opportunity to remind me of the old Russell who was driven, judgmental, and miserable. For some, there was a value in seeing what I was like so they would not have to experience it themselves.

Rather than regretting the time lost with my children when they were young, I find comfort in the knowledge that I can now spend time with them, and that they know firsthand the value of being with family. The lesson was for me as well as my children. Perhaps my lesson will result in their spending time with their children when they are young. If so, I have benefited my children's children.

As we are all one, what we do to one we do to ourselves. We allow and participate in what happens to us at the hands of others and vice versa.

Make a list of all your regrets over the years from an early age until now. The length will amaze you, and it will stir up old emotions. Allow them and feel them. Then write down the lessons learned from the regrets and how they have helped you or made you a better person today.

Do not regret. Be pleased with the lesson, the learning, and the growth. When you feel regret, look deep within it. What is the lesson? What is the value? How did it or will it help you or the other person involved?

Who Am I?

"I don't know who my grandfather was. I am much more concerned to know who his grandson will be." Abraham Lincoln

Am I my physical body? (such as tall, dark, and handsome)
Am I my mental ability? (such as rocket scientist)
Am I my position at work? (such as customer service representative)
Am I my heritage? (such as Indian)
Am I my unique ability? (such as violinist)
Am I my family? (such as mother of six children)
Am I my ego? (such as greater than others)

I am an eternal soul that has taken on a physical earthly body to learn some lessons and help others learn. I am part of all that is. I am vibration and light. I am no better and no worse than anyone else. I am the sum total of all I have learned.

We need to look inside ourselves to see who we are. Superficially, many of us show others that we fit into society and the norms expected of us. We are not the exterior that others see. The exterior might be a business suit or a uniform. We are not our job, our position, our profession, or our family. We are not the role we play on the stage of earth.

Our problems, our conflicts, and our fear all come from being someone we are not. We are not our role. We are not our ego. We need to be who we truly are while also playing this game called life on earth. We are eternal beings having an earth experience, learning and growing.

I am one, and we are all one. We are connected. You are part of me, and I am part of you.

Success

At times, winning can mean losing and losing can mean winning.

What is success for you? Is success the amount of money you earn? Is it a bigger better house in the right part of town? Is it a new car? Is it a new boat? Is it a ski house? Is it having the socially acceptable partner?

If so, why do you feel empty? Why do those things lose their luster when attained? Why are they never enough?

Too often success means chasing the external things, such as cars and other status symbols. These things are of earth and not of lasting value. Most of our symbols of success on earth are things that rust, age, burn, and are destroyed over time. When we leave this earthly life, we do not take these things with us. As we are dying our earthly death, I dare say none of the above matters.

True success is knowing who you are and why you are here. It is connecting with a soul mate. It is helping others and seeing the joy of accomplishment on another person's face. It is a deep and powerful connection with all that is. It is making the world a better place for our children and our children's children. We create our success by following our life's purpose.

Success is found within. It is eternal and long lasting. You take this type of success with you as you transition out of this earthly life. Material success on earth is short-lived and never truly satisfying.

For me, success and happiness are having children who enjoy my company and like doing things with me. It is their phone calls. It is being together and doing nothing. It is the memories of bike rides and vacations. It is looking forward to the next family trip.

"Bebo" is the affectionate name we called my father-in-law. He was in the navy for twenty years. He retired and delivered mail on a rural route in Saunderstown, Rhode Island. Then he retired a second time and worked for the church before his final retirement and move to Florida. During this period he was involved in the Kentish Guards, the Lions, the American Legion, the Irish American Club, and many other organizations. He always ended up as president and running the organizations. We also called him the "grand pooh-bah." While he never earned a lot of money, he always had enough to care for his family and enjoy himself.

His funeral was a big event. His success could be measured in the number of friends paying their respects. Many arrived with stories of how he had enriched their lives and how he would be missed. He was a success and spread goodwill to others. His sense of humor was legendary. A friend's wife said she visited him in the hospital right after she had had her hair done. She walked in the room looking good, and he immediately asked, "Weren't you going to get your hair done?" Only Bebo could get away with a comment like that and make everyone laugh.

Tim Russert, journalist and host of NBC's *Meet the Press,* wrote a book called *Big Russ and Me* about his life with his father. Big Russ worked for the sanitation department and held a second job driving a delivery truck. Russert wrote the book to tell of the life lessons and values he had learned from his father. Perhaps part of the reason the book was a best seller is that it shows us the great value that can be created by anyone from any walk of life. Big Russ is truly successful. He created value and lives a life of contribution and value even if he did not earn a lot of money.

May we all be as successful as Bebo and Big Russ.

Abundance Worth Having

If you were given six months to live, what would you do with your time? You would probably make valuable use of every minute, not to gain material wealth but to spend and enrich your time with family and friends.

Most people dream of a life of abundance with houses, cars, toys, and trips. These material things are valued and make us feel good.

Many feel abundant when they are able to purchase what they want, show off their new purchases, and talk of their latest trips. They strive to do better than the family next door or others at the club.

Sometimes friends are valued based on what they have and do. Jealousy may be part of it, but many people seek the status of being friendly with wealthy people.

Many people work hard to climb that slippery ladder of success. At times some people are fearful of the new day and the challenges. Will we earn what we need, will we get the promotion, or will we get hired? How can we save face? How can we make it look good to our peers?

People often focus on the abundance of things, positions held, associations based on money, board seats, and community respect. Occasionally people will even go into debt for the abundance of things.

Some people tire of the game, and the fun is gone. They have worked and worked and are burnt out. The value is gone, but the debts still continue. They wonder if this abundance, this game, is all there is to life. The fun and excitement are long past.

What is it they were after? Did they succeed? Is this all there is? What do we have to look forward to? Does the game ever end?

Can we ever win the game of money? The more we work, the more we spend, and the more we look around and compare. Someone has made millions and is the new envy of the neighborhood. Someone else bought the newest toy, and we wonder who will be next and if we should buy one also.

If you are tired of this rat race, this money game, this trying to keep up with and ahead of the Joneses, it might be time to redefine "abundance."

The *Oxford American Dictionary and Thesaurus* definition of abundance is:
1. a very great quantity, considered to be more than enough; 2. wealth; affluence; 3. wealth of emotion (abundance of heart); 4. overflow, superfluity, excess, surplus, too much, oversupply, glut

To me, abundance is what you take with you when you die. The principles are as follows:

<u>Abundance is joy and freedom.</u>

Money is only one small part of abundance, but it gets the most attention. Remember, the stuff that money buys rusts, burns, gets stolen, or wears out. The newest and greatest car today is outdated in a few years. The big house is not only expensive to buy but also draining to care for and ties you down.

Look at all your stuff that represents abundance. Is the big house worth it? Is it fun, or is it a drain? Are the three cars worth the cost and effort? Does it feel good to spend $75,000 on a car? Does the car give you that much value and satisfaction? See what you have that you do not use or enjoy. Should you sell it or give it away? Would your life be better or worse without the stuff?

Joy comes from within. Money creates a temporary false happiness but not joy. Freedom is a state of mind and a way of life. Stuff can overshadow your freedom and occupy your time.

<u>Abundance is stuff.</u>

Now is the time to look at the abundance of stuff. The idea is to use it, love it, or lose it. If you have not used it in a year and do not love it, perhaps it is time to lose it.

Get fifty storage boxes. Start with the clothes closets. Take the items that no longer fit, have not been worn in years, or are out of style, and give them away. There are many people who will use your old clothes. You do not need them, will not use them, and they are cluttering your home and space. For those that you do wear, put the seasonal clothes in boxes marked accordingly. Keep in the closet only what you are currently wearing. Leave room. A crowded, cluttered closet can make you feel crowded and cluttered mentally and emotionally.

Next, the basement. Do you have grown children's possessions still stored in your house? Tell them to come and get them. If they do not claim their stuff within an allotted time, give it away. If they want to keep it but don't have room, perhaps you will allow them to pack and label it for storage in your basement.

For the stuff you feel you must keep but do not anticipate using, box it and record what is in each box. After several years of not opening the box, it will be time to throw it away. It is an ongoing process. Today is the beginning. As time goes on, you will be able to discard more and more. Now we are working with the tip of the iceberg.

Next attack the garage and attic, as well as any outbuilding.

<u>Abundance is time.</u>

Let's assume we have sixteen hours a day and seven days a week. How do we spend that time? Assess how you spend your time in the following areas:

Work
Family activities (dinner, theater, barbecues, etc.)
Being together as a couple
Social fun time
Social obligations—not fun
Community meetings—groups that are enjoyable and fun
Community meetings—groups that are not fun
Educational (learning new things—books, courses, workshops)

Household chores (cleaning, shopping, mowing the lawn, gardening)

Look over the list and notice how your time balances out. Is there enough time for family? Is there enough time for being together? Is there enough time for doing fun things? Is there too much time spent on stuff that is not fun and doesn't add value? Are there things you need to or want to eliminate? Are there groups that no longer hold interest for you? Are there activities that are no longer fun? Are there old relationships that are long gone but on which you still spend time begrudgingly? How much time is spent on "shoulds" that are not enjoyable? Are there things you do to enable others that hurt them and you?

Too often we race from one thing to the next never doing justice to anything. Now that you have reduced what you spend your time on, it is time to add abundance to what is left.

<u>Abundance is family.</u>

For most of us, the family is the most important unit. Face-to-face time and quality time is what counts. Sitting in front of the TV, a short distracted phone call, and a quick meal at a drive-through restaurant do not count.

Relationships take time. It is the time together, the doing and being available for another that creates and promotes love and respect. One cannot speed up or take shortcuts in relationships. It is about making memories of things done and time spent together. It is the joy of being with a loved one.

<u>Abundance is close friends, employees, and clients.</u>

It is the relationships with others you truly like—close friends, club members, business associates, etc.—that enrich your life.

Now is the time to look around and expand your vision. Who else can use your attention, your gifts of time and talent, as well as your expertise? Who can you help? Who can you guide? Who can you mentor? And who can help you?

Abundance is time spent with others in order to truly know them and to give to them, be it for profit, nonprofit, or fun. It is time to pay attention to them, assist them, and allow yourself to be assisted by them. By investing time and talent, you will build relationships of lasting value. You will feel abundant. It is the abundance of knowing you helped, you added value, and you made another's burdens a little lighter for them.

Abundance is giving back.

Make a list of the abundance that has been given to you by others. You may be embarrassed to discover how much you've been given and how little you may have given back. You will see and notice people and actions that were, in fact, gifts that you did not have the presence of mind to recognize or to give back to them. It is okay. In giving to others, we need not get back from them. In receiving we need not necessarily give back to them. In receiving we give, and in giving we receive. The giving is also a gift to us. In giving we feel abundant. In giving we are satisfied. In giving we learn that we are meant to give, and we experience the joy that it brings to us.

As Ralph Waldo Emerson said, "It is one of the most beautiful compensations of this life that no man can sincerely try to help another without helping himself."

Abundance is learning, education, and skills.

Make a list now of what you would like to learn. It may be education classes or hands-on skills you have always wanted. Make it fun. Do not restrict or censor your list. If belly dancing is a secret desire, list it. If being a Chippendale is a secret desire, list it.

Then pursue these dreams. Find the class. Find the course. Find the tutors. It is time for the abundance of doing, learning, and adding skills. This will benefit not only you but also others. This is something for you, and what benefits you can also benefit others.

Abundance is free time.

Abundance can be found in travel. Make a list of the places where you have always wanted to go and visit at least one a year. Also, do at least one short excursion every month. It can be for an hour, a full day, or overnight.

For some, free time is best enjoyed being at home playing games or involved in a hobby. Others may enjoy a long leisurely walk along a wooded path. We all have our own special ways to use and enjoy the abundance of free time. The key is to make time for what you enjoy that adds value to your life.

<u>Abundance is money.</u>

Money is the medium we use for exchange. That is all that it is. We use money as a means of barter.

Abundance is having enough money. The issue is what is enough money? "Enough" varies, based on the person's perceptions.

There is nothing wrong with money, nice houses, nice cars, and nice toys, but at what price do we need them? How much time must you commit to work in order to buy something? Is that "something" worth the time it takes to get it? If so, then do it. If not, don't do it. Do not allow money and the stuff it buys to occupy your time. Do not be a slave to your money and stuff.

<u>Abundance is what you take with you when you die.</u>

On your deathbed, your biggest regrets will be things not experienced, risks not taken, and time wasted. When you die, you cannot take your stuff with you. (Although some people have actually been buried in their cars.) But, in reality, nothing of material value can go with you. The house, the car, the boat, and the golf clubs have no value to you when you die.

So, what do you take with you? The abundance of peace of mind knowing you lived an honorable life, that you gave of yourself to family and friends, and that you left your community and the world better places.

Living My Life

"...cause and effect is as absolute and undeviating in the hidden realm of thought as in the world of visible and material things.... The mind is the master weaver, both of the inner garment of character and the outer garment of circumstance..."
James Allen

The key to a fulfilling life is to make and live the life you want with ease, abundance, and confidence.

To do this we need to know, understand, and apply simple and effective principles.

We are the masters of our own fates. We have a conscious mind and a subconscious mind. We make up our own truth, and then we believe it. This is why honest people can have different views of the truth in any given situation. To them, their own individual view is the truth, and they have made it true for themselves.

We are all one. We are all connected. While this may sound and feel strange to you, it is true. Have you ever known what someone was thinking? Have you ever known who was calling before you answered the phone? Have you ever felt you knew someone you just met? These phenomena occur because we are connected. There is communication on another level, on another plane, that we are not consciously aware of.

As inside, so outside. Our external world and environment, as well as our friends and relationships, are a reflection of our inside. If we are at peace inside, if we are in harmony with all that is, if we respect and enjoy all that is, our outside world will be peaceful and in harmony also. If our inside is full of hate and hostility, that is the environment we have chosen, and it will be reflected in the area where we live and the people with whom we associate.

To change the outside, we need to change the inside first. The inside is the cause, and the outside is the effect. It is useless to try to change the outside first, because it does not work. The effort is on the inside. Change the beliefs, change the truth, and the outside will change automatically.

A flower never seems to have to work at blossoming. It just does. That is because the work is inside, and the outside is just a reflection of the inside. If we get the inside right, the outside will be right also.

The mind provides the truth as we know it to the subconscious, which does the work. The subconscious maintains our breathing day and night, keeping the blood flowing and all the bodily functions in order every minute of our lives.

The conscious mind is the space where we design the life we want and where we decide on health or sickness. The focused proper thoughts are our truth, which the subconscious accepts and then produces the results. If we think negative thoughts and feel hostility, our body will become negative and blocked. A negative and blocked body will be a sick body.

If we give positive thoughts to the subconscious, it will provide positive results. However, these cannot be scattered thoughts that change each hour or day. The subconscious creates what we think and feel on a regular basis. It creates what we repeat. We think it and repeat it until it becomes the truth for us. The subconscious believes it and creates it for us in the outer world.

What is the power of the subconscious mind? The power is that it is one with all that is. It is part of the one mind that exists in the universe and has access to it. We need only to properly direct the subconscious, and it can then bring to us the people, the places, and the things we so desire. The subconscious can bring to us the abundance of all that is.

The subconscious mind does not judge. It accepts what the conscious mind gives it and then creates it in the universe. It gives back to us what we give to it. The more focus, the more positive thoughts, and the more love and emotion we provide, the greater and faster the results.

The key is to think the thoughts that we want and not to dwell on what we do not want. If we think lack, there will be lack. If we think hate, there will be hate. If we think we can't, we won't. If we think we can, we will. If we love and respect, we will get love and respect.

Negative thoughts and emotions are like weeds in a garden. The weeds can overtake and kill the plant. Do not let the weeds in your mind take control and choke the life out of what you desire. Use the mind to make a clear and conscious vision of what you want and hold that vision as it becomes realized. Eliminate the negative destructive thoughts as you would pull weeds out of your garden.

In order to get, we need to give. When we give, we get back what we give. The more we give, the more we get. If we give negative hateful thoughts and comments, they will come back to us. If we treat people with respect and kindness, we will get that back. We only need to see how people treat us, and we will see how we are treating them. As you sow, so shall you reap.

If you do not like your life, your circumstances, or associates, change. The key is to change in your mind first. See and focus on what you truly want, make that your truth, and in time the subconscious will create it in your outside world. Your environment and friends can and will change. As with a plant, the growth is not immediate. Plant the seeds in your mind, nurture and feed them with proper positive thoughts, and focus. The thoughts will produce the desired results. The time will depend upon your focus and the nature of your thoughts.

Create the life you want in your mind, visualize it, focus on it, know it to be true, and know the subconscious mind is creating it and bringing it into your physical world.

Climb the Right Mountain

"To thine own self be true ..." William Shakespeare

What mountain are you climbing? Why? Are you doing your life's work? Are you happy with your work? Are you happy with your life?

Are you doing what others feel you should do? Are you in a job you don't like, but you fear the risk of change? Are you afraid of what others might say? Are you afraid you might not be successful?

Many times we do what others think we should do. Too often people do not follow their inner urgings. We must do what is right for us. We must do what we came to earth to do.

Our mountain might change. We might find the mountain is the wrong one. If we are not satisfied with or motivated by our work, or if we dread it, we might be climbing the wrong mountain.

We should approach each day with excitement and look forward to our potential accomplishments. Every day should hold some opportunity to learn and grow. It might be as simple as an interaction with a coworker. It might be giving encouragement to someone.

We should not be working for money alone. We should not be working for acceptance. We should not be working in a job we hate because the family expects us to do so. We should not be doing what we do not like because it is expected of us by society.

We need to be true to our mission and our purpose. We need to be true to our inner soul and what it tells us. We need to do what we fear so we can get to what we need to do. We need self-acceptance first. In losing ourselves through serving others, we will find ourselves.

"If you were not paid, would you still do the work you are doing now?" I was asked. "Of course not," I replied. "Then, why are you doing it?" was the next question. Facing the truth in ourselves is not always easy, but it sure is effective. Climb the right mountain.

Now

"And if not now, when?" Talmud

Now is all we have. Now is all we will ever have. Now is all we ever had. Tomorrow never comes. The past is gone.

This moment is all there is. We need to learn to be in the moment. Often we are numb to the moment because we are living with a past memory or thinking of what we need to do later. Dwelling on the past or the future does not allow us to be fully in the moment. We miss what is going on. We are stressed, worried, and preoccupied.

Peace, relaxation, and focus can only be accomplished when you are in the now. The past is gone, and the future never comes. Give your full attention to the moment and what you are doing. That way you will be able to do your best, and you will enjoy what you are doing.

Do what needs to be done now. Tomorrow never comes. If it is worth doing, it is worth doing now. Why delay? If it is of value, then do it. If you wait, you stand a better chance of not getting around to it. If you wait, you will delay the benefit of what you were going to do.

Are you climbing the right mountain? Are you satisfied and fulfilled? Stop, listen, feel, allow the discomfort, look within, look in the dark corners, and the truth that you already know will be waiting for you. Now is the time to find and climb the right mountain.

Now is the best time for interaction. We do not know when a loved one will cross over. If we want to speak to them in the human form, we need to do it today. If it is on our minds, it very likely will be on their minds also. Why not address it with words? Subconsciously we have already spoken and connected. However, it is also of great value to connect with words. If we do it now, we can reap the benefits longer. If we do it now, we can all feel better now. If we do it now, we do not have to worry about doing it in the future.

When you finish reading this book, it is not done and over. The end of the book is the beginning. It is the beginning of reflecting on it and rereading it. The second time you will obtain far more insight than the first time. Your true self will shine through more and more each time you read it.

Finally, you will begin. You will face your true self, and you will face your fear. You will do what you fear because you know it is right for you. The key is to do it now, when you know it is right, and not delay it for the tomorrow that never comes.

Do it now.

My Message

"Whatever you can do, or dream you can, begin it. Boldness has genius, power and magic in it." Johann Wolfgang von Goethe

Sit quietly. Feel, allow, and know. Listen to your body. Listen to your intuitive connection with all that is. Listen with your heart and not your mind. Be still. Take your time in reading this last chapter. There is no rush.

Past history is a basis for learning and understanding but not for regrets. You can't change the past. You can learn from it. Your past changes according to your filters, your learning, and your emotions of the moment. What is real to one is not real to another. Each person's view and reality is different based on their filters.

Our past history, our learning, and our perceptions all create filters for us. We all see the same facts a little or a lot differently from one another. Today the reality of my childhood experiences is different than it was years ago. Look at the positive lessons you have learned. They may have taught you what not to do after having seen a parent do it. Appreciate the past and know it was as it needed to be.

Only in giving do we receive. Our true value and true self-worth have everything to do with giving of ourselves for others. It is only in the giving that we truly receive. Learn and know the true joy of giving. In losing ourselves through helping others, we find ourselves.

Giving starts with the family. To whom have you given the least? For many of us, it is our spouse and children, as well as our parents. While there may not be public recognition, fame, and glory in giving at home, that is where we should start.

Do not regret what you have not done. *Now* is the time to do what you know to be right.

Kiss and be kissed. Hold hands and be held. Pay attention and be paid attention to. Cathy has taught me that you get what you give. At times that has not been fun and occasionally downright painful. As soon as we take someone for granted or ignore them, we lose.

Do what you fear and the death of the fear is certain. Follow your gut, follow your inner urgings, trust yourself, and follow the desires and needs of your spirit. Don't follow your ego. Don't follow what others say you should do. Don't follow society and what makes you fit in or look good. Do what you know you need to do. Do what has passion, meaning, and purpose for you. We have to get out of our own way to allow God within to guide us. If you can dream it or think it, you can do it.

Reflect on the balance in life. Reflect on how things work out and how what you need is there exactly when you need it—not before and not after.

Stop, think, and remember a serious event in the past. In that moment it may have seemed that the world would come to an end. Now fast-forward to the results of how it worked out. It may have worked out for the better. It may have changed the course of your history. The point is that things happen, and then there is a new and different balance. When one thing leaves, another appears. Remember, when a door closes, a window opens. If there is no door or window, make one.

Look within to contact your deep inner being. Be quiet, reflect, meditate, and study your inner feelings and emotions. They are sending you messages. Fear, anger, dissatisfaction, and frustration are signs of one's need to look within. Relationships turned bad are messages. It is all about you and your reaction to people and events. It is not them; it is your reaction to them.

Fear is of earth and of not knowing. Confidence is allowing the God within you to do and to act. Confidence is knowing within yourself that you can do something. You build confidence by doing something and repeating it. The confidence with which you approach and do something gives you the power and ability to accomplish it. Remember, "I can if I think I can." It is that simple. Confidence is from God within.

While here, you can certainly enjoy the pleasures of earth and physical possessions. Just don't make them your gods or reasons for being and doing. The physical possessions are part of the game, and if you play the game with love in your heart and assist others, there is nothing wrong with enjoying the physical assets. The goal needs to be the process and not the end result, the material possessions, or the ego gratification.

If you lack purpose in life, if attaining your goals leaves you empty, and if there is no joy in your life, then look within. These feelings are telling you a change is needed. The feelings are your guides to assist you in finding your path. Follow your true path, not the path of the ego, not the path of "should," and not the path of the socially acceptable. Follow your true inner path. You will find the reason you are here, your purpose that will fill you and your life with joy.

If you did not get paid for what you do, would you do it? If not, it's the wrong job. Do what you love, what provides joy to you and value to others. The money will take care of itself.

When you leave this earthly school, what will you take with you? Love, relationships, lessons learned, lessons attempted, and lessons ignored. Please know that for those things not done or not done well enough, you will be back again to continue the task. There is no time limit or number of lives necessary to learn your lessons. However, why not become more enlightened this time and improve your progress? Reading this book is not a coincidence. You are reading this book for a purpose: to help you on your path. I'm here to help you, and you're here to help me. It is not up to us to judge who we help or to judge the quality or value of our help.

The Ten Rules:

1. Let go and let God.

2. Love God.

3. Love your neighbor as yourself.

4.   Love your father and mother.

5.   Die now so you know there is no death.

6.   The secret to living is giving.

7.   As you sow, so shall you reap.

8.   Be present, be in the moment, be in the *now*.

9.   It's the process, the journey, and the learning, not the end result.

10. We are all *one*.

In that we are all one, why not do what you are meant to do? Why not take the risk to do what you feel is right? Why not be the best you can be? Why worry about what others will think when you are a mirror to help them learn? Why not give freely of yourself, as in giving you will receive?

Write your obituary. Write it *now*. Then review it. Are you satisfied? Does it represent a life well lived and shared? If not, then write the obituary you wish it to be. Then, today, start to live that life, so it will be as you desire. Yes, today you can take the first step.

We have met and will meet again. The work and the journey belong to all of us. It is time to live the life you are meant to live. It is time to give yourself permission to act, to do, to be, to know, and to feel. Dare to be the best you can be. Dare to follow your heart. Dare to do what you know is right for you.

Epilogue

I can feel it now. The book is public, and I am at risk. More than one friend may say, "He doesn't walk the talk." Others will say, "I know mistakes he has made." Still others will say, "He's sure not perfect." Still others might not be as kind. They are all right.

When Cathy finished the book, she asked me, "Why don't you live your learning?" I am. I am doing my best; and that is better than I was doing and not as good as I will be doing.

Cathy would confirm that I am not a saint. I still get upset. I still judge. I am still a fallen pilgrim who is learning. We all are faced with lessons daily. We handle some better than others. I am aware that those I still do not handle properly will come back again until I do.

I know there is a reason, a purpose, and a value in what happens. I am learning to stop and look at the situation as if it is a play on a stage. That way, a little removed, I have a better vision of it all and can see the lesson in it. The trick is to not jump into the heat of the battle with my ego and judgment before I sit back and view the situation from a distance with the advantage of my learning.

Recommended Reading

The Alchemist by Paulo Coelho

As a Man Thinketh by James Allen

Ask and It Is Given by Esther and Jerry Hicks

A Course in Miracles by Foundation for Inner Peace

The Disappearance of the Universe by Gary Renard

The Four Agreements by Don Miguel Ruiz

The Holy Bible

The Isaiah Effect by Gregg Braden

The Master Key System by Charles F. Haanel

The Power of Intention by Dr. Wayne Dyer

The Power of Now by Eckhart Tolle

Power vs. Force by Dr. David R. Hawkins

The Sedona Method by Hale Dwoskin

The Seven Spiritual Laws of Success by Deepak Chopra, MD

Walking Between the Worlds by Gregg Braden

You Can Heal Your Life by Louise Hay

www.ourjourneyisourwork.com

978-0-595-40349-3
0-595-40349-2

Printed in the United States
64379LVS00006B/424-549

9 780595 403493